Serial K[illegible] Quotes

Inside the Minds of Murderers

by

Benjamin James

ISBN: 1726415759
ISBN-13: 978-1726415750

First Edition

FOREWARD

In addition to covering just the standard serial killers in this book, you will also find quotes and musings from mass murderers, spree killers, cult leaders and cult members. To compare and contrast the mindset of different types of killers, a great effort has been made to provide the most accurate transcriptions possible.

The views and opinions expressed in this book
do not necessarily reflect those of the author or the publisher.

For all those who never stopped seeking knowledge.
Keep seeking.

For all those who never gave up on their dreams.
Keep dreaming.

CONTENTS

"I was born with the devil in me. I could not help the fact that I was a murderer, no more than the poet can help the inspiration to sing.

I was born with the evil one standing as my sponsor beside the bed where I was ushered into the world, and he has been with me since."

H.H. Holmes

"May your wife and children get raped, right in the ass."

Aileen Wuornos

"Do I look like someone who cares about
what God thinks?"

Elizabeth Bathory

"I just liked to kill, I wanted to kill."

Ted Bundy

"I shot a guy one time in his Adam's apple to see how long it would take him to die."

Richard Kuklinski

"I am waiting for a good movie about me. Who will play me? I am now in control of all things."

The Zodiac Killer

"The sixth commandment, 'Thou Shalt Not Kill' fascinated me. I always knew that some day I should defy it."

John Reginald Halliday Christie

"We wanted to do a crime that the world would have to stand up and take notice."

Susan Atkins

"A clown can get away with murder."

John Wayne Gacy

"If you lift the soap and find that underneath it is dry, you're alright. If it's gooey, you have the poisoning, which turns your blood to powder. The powder then depletes your energy and eats away at your body."

Richard Trenton Chase

"I always wondered what it would be like to kill someone."

Gary Ridgeway (Green River Killer)

"I just wanted to see how it felt to shoot Grandma."

Edmund Kemper

"My cross in my bedroom still has the flowers that I slipped into Jesus's feet when Susan Atkins died. I cried a tear and I asked for forgiveness on Susan Atkins soul. I'll do the same thing when Charlie dies."

Leslie Van Houten

"To me death is not a fearful thing. It's living that's cursed."

Jim Jones

"I couldn't find any meaning for my life when I was out there. I'm sure as hell not going to find it in here. This is the grand finale of a life poorly spent and the end result is just overwhelmingly depressing.

It's just a sick, pathetic, wretched, miserable life story. That's all it is. How it can help anyone, I've no idea."

Jeffery Dahmer

"They say it's the number of people I killed, I say it's the principle."

Aileen Wuornos

"Obviously and logically, I wish to end it. I have, in effect, been kept in suspended animation since 1965."

Ian Brady

"You feel the last bit of breath leaving their body.
You're looking into their eyes.
A person in that situation is God."

Ted Bundy

"I followed the woman from the convenience store to a driveway she pulled into. And I hung around several hours, till it come wee hours of the morning.

Then I went into this house. I go to the first bedroom. I see... I don't know whose room it is and, and, and, and I start stabbing."

Tommy Lynn Sells

"None of us are saints."

Albert Fish

"When I didn't kill, I would get nervous. I would pace around the house, and then when I killed, it calmed me."

Pedro Rodrigues Filho

"Hello from the gutters of New York City, which are filled with dog manure, vomit, stale wine, urine and blood."

David Berkowitz

"Assassin... sounds so exotic. I was just a murderer."

Richard Kuklinski

"If you're talking about the Summerdale house and the bodies found there, we feel that some of them died of drug overdose, then buried alive.

Trouble is the state never did toxicology on the victims, as they wouldn't fit with their theory that they were all strangled."

John Wayne Gacy

"People don't know me. They think they do, but they don't."

Andrew Cunanan

"Even when she was dead, she was still bitching at me.
I couldn't get her to shut up."

Edmund Kemper

"Killing is killing whether done for duty, profit or fun."

Richard Ramirez

"She was giving me oral sex and she got carried away, so I choked her."

Arthur Shawcross

“They're daring me to kill again."

Aileen Wuornos

"People don't appreciate life. To be more sensitive they have to see horrors. I'm the horror who forces people to try to live differently."

Anatoly Onoprienko

"Do I look like the Green River Killer?"

Gary Ridgeway (Green River Killer)

"Give a bitch a choice between getting dicked and getting hurt. You know what she's gonna pick."

Bobby Joe Long

"We have no sympathy in killing humans who have no respect for other people's lives."

Seung Hui Cho

"In my dream I see before me a forest of crucifixes which gradually turn into trees. At first there appears to be dew or rain dripping from the branches, but as I approach, I realize it is blood.

Suddenly the whole forest begins to writhe. The trees, stark and erect, ooze blood. A man goes to each tree catching the blood in a cup. When his cup is full he approaches me. "Drink," he says. But I am unable to move."

John Haigh

“I saw the surprise, the shock, the blank... they're gone. And all I saw was my reflection. That's it.”

Richard Kuklinski

"My consuming lust was to experience their bodies. I viewed them as objects, as strangers. It is hard for me to believe a human being could have done what I've done."

Jeffery Dahmer

“We do in all honesty hate this world.”

Marshall Applewhite

"There is no happiness without tears,no life without death. Beware! I am going to make you cry."

Lucian Staniak

"Kill one and you might as well kill 21."

Mark Martin

"I shan't shed a tear. Life is full of shocks of all descriptions and they have to be faced."

Patrick Mackay

"Anybody can kill anybody."

Lynette "Squeaky" Fromme

"In my lifetime I have broken every law that was ever made by both man and God. If either had made any more, I should very cheerfully have broken them also."

Carl Panzram

"When I killed people I had a desire. This inspired me to kill more. I don't care if they deserve to live or not"

Yang Xahai

"If I killed them, you know, they couldn't reject me as a man. It was more or less making a doll out of a human being and carrying out my fantasies with a doll, a living human doll."

Edmund Kemper

"Most of the people at the ranch were just people you did not want, people that were alongside the road."

Charles Manson

"You maggots make me sick, I will be avenged.
Lucifer dwells within us all."

Richard Ramirez

"I wish I could live it all over again."

Richard Marquette

"I always had a fetish for murder and death."

David Berkowitz

"I actually think I may be possessed with demons. I was dropped on my head as a kid."

Dennis Rader (BTK)

"What I did was not for sexual pleasure.
Rather it brought me some peace of mind."

Andrei Chikatilo

“"Hey mom. Gotta go. It's about a half an hour before our little judgment day. I just wanted to apologize to you guys for any crap this might instigate.”

Dylan Klebold

"To me, this world is nothing but evil and my own evil just happened to come out 'cause of the circumstances of what I was doing."

Aileen Wuornos

"I did this not as a sex act...but out of hate for her. I don't mean out of hate for her in particular, really I mean out of hate for a woman."

Albert DeSalvo

"That is my ambition, to have killed more people, more helpless people, than any man or woman who has ever lived."

Jane Toppan

"I carried it too far, that's for sure. "

Jeffery Dahmer

"If you don't kill me, you're stupid... because the next time you see me, I will kill you."

Richard Kuklinski

"We all go a little mad sometimes."

Ted Bundy

"You eat meat with your teeth and you kill things that are better than you are, and in the same respect you say how bad and even killers that your children are.

You make your children what they are."

Charles Manson

"I believe the only way to reform people is to kill them"
Carl Panzram"

"Uh, you all haven't asked this, but I will go ahead and tell you this. Do I think I'm the one that killed this kid? Yes. Uh, if it wasn't this kid I killed, then there's a murder out there that, that we still ain't undug yet."

Tommy Lynn Sells

"I had an unspeakable delight in strangling women, experiencing during the act erections and real sexual pleasure. The feeling of pleasure while strangling them was much greater than that which I experienced while masturbating.

It never occurred to me to touch or look at the genitals. It satisfied me to seize the women by the neck and suck their blood. "

Vincenz Verzeni

"If the blue meanies are going to get me they'd better get off their asses and do something."

The Zodiac Killer

It wasn't as dark and scary as it sounds. I had a lot of fun. Killing somebody's a funny experience."

Albert DeSalvo

"The Summerdale house is rented to PDM contractors. There was 12 keys out to it. But that was never allowed to come out at the trial as it would put doubt in the states theory. They didn't want anybody to know that people had keys to the house.

Plus the fact that I wasn't always at the house, so others used it just as much, and again that wasn't brought out at the trial as it didn't fit with the states theory of the case that I committed all the crime."

John Wayne Gacy

"The hand that pulled the trigger that killed your sons now masturbates to the memory. Fuck all of you."

T.J. Lane

"Death is only the beginning.
In Death I find hope,
the hope of better times,
of no memories,
of forgiveness, gotten and given.
In Death I can see my kids,
I can tell them that I am sorry
and that I love them.
No more pain, guilt or shame.
In Death, I will be able to
Breathe Again.
Death is welcomed, is needed
is longed for.
Death is only the beginning."

Dale S. Hausner

"I always had the desire to inflict pain on others and to have others inflict pain on me. I always seemed to enjoy everything that hurt. The desire to inflict pain, that is all that is uppermost. "

Albert Fish

"When I murdered my wife I removed the one obstacle which for ten years had apparently held me in check.

After she had gone, the way was clear for me to fulfill my destiny."

John Reginald Halliday Christie

"Satan gets into people and makes them do things they don't want to."

Herbert Mullin

"The only thing they can get me for is running a funeral parlor without a license."

John Wayne Gacy

"You learn what you need to kill and take care of the details. It's like changing a tire.

The first time you're careful. By the thirtieth time, you can't remember where you left the lug wrench"

Ted Bundy

"It tries to think for me. It says it will kill me if it gets me."

Kenneth Erskine

"I don't lose sleep over what I have done or have nightmares about it."

Dennis Nilsen

"You won't find any woman who'll say anything other than that I was always a perfect gentleman in their presence."

Charles Albright

"Believe me, if I started murdering people, there'd be none of you left."

Charles Manson

"If I gave a shit about the parents I wouldn't have killed the kid."

Clifford Olson

"After my head has been chopped off, will I still be able to hear, at least for a moment, the sound of my own blood gushing from my neck?

That would be the best pleasure to end all pleasure."

Peter Kurten

"I've killed 20 people, man. I love all that blood."

Richard Ramirez

“I'm not looking for forgiveness and I'm not repenting.”

Richard Kuklinski

"When the circumstances are right,

everything becomes a dance."

Lynette "Squeaky" Fromme

"The first good-looking girl I see tonight is going to die."

Edmund Kemper

"Every man to his own tastes. Mine is for corpses."

Henri Blot

"I hated all my life. I hated everybody. When I first grew up and can remember, I was dressed as a girl by mother.

And I stayed that way for two or three years. And after that was treated like what I call the dog of the family.

I was beaten. I was made to do things that no human being would want to do."

Henry Lee Lucas

"When you work hard to do something right, you don't want to forget it."

Ted Bundy

"I may be a bit peculiar."

George Jospeh Smith

"I just didn't care anymore and I wanted to stop.
I was sick inside."

Bobby Joe Long

"I am not insane, I'm just queer."

Albert Fish

"Kill for my masters."

David Berkowitz

"It is true to say that I was nurtured on Bible stories but mostly concerned with sacrifice. If by some mischance I did or said anything which my father regarded as improper, he would say: 'Do not grieve the Lord by behaving so.'

And if I suggested that I wanted to go somewhere, or meet somebody, he would say: 'It will not please the Lord."

John Haigh

"They were themselves to blame if I had to shoot them."

Klaus Gossman

"What I did is not such a great harm, with all these surplus women nowadays. Anyway, I had a good time."

Rudolf Pleil

"I simulate various future scenarios relating to resistance efforts, confrontations with police, future interrogation scenarios, future court appearances, future media interviews, etc."

Anders Breivik

"I saw so many boys whipped, it took root in my head."

Albert Fish

"When I saw her for the first time I had an idea to strangle her."

Gennady Mikhasevich

"We serial killers are your sons, we are your husbands, we are everywhere, and there will be more of your children dead tomorrow."

Ted Bundy

"There was no smell. Over the years time other than when it rained, the musty odor was present. People were in and out of that house daily for years. And other than when it rained, there was no odor and certainly not like what some of the books said.

That's all fantasy. If that odor was there somebody would have noticed it sooner."

John Wayne Gacy

"Contrary to popular perception, the so-called Moors Murders were merely an existential exercise of just over a year, which was concluded in December 1964."

Ian Brady

"It was an urge, a strong urge, and the longer I let it go, the stronger it got, to where I was taking risks to go out and kill people, risks that normally, according to my little rules of operation, I wouldn't take because they could lead to arrest."

Edmund Kemper

"I took the right leg of that woman's body. From the knee to the hip, took the fat off and ate it while he stared at the other girl. When I bit into it she just urinated right there."

Arthur Shawcross

"I went in and, and, and I don't know if it was her room,
don't know if it was his room, I don't, I just knew
I wanted to go in there and, and hurt someone."

Tommy Lynn Sells

"I've got to start eating at home more."

Jeffery Dahmer

"You could be at home right now eating your fucking caviar and your fucking cognac, had you not ravenously raped my soul."

Seung Hui Cho

"He started messing with the Christmas tree, telling me how nice the Christmas tree was. So I shot him."

David Bullock

"Well first off I disagree with the state theory. As I think all they looked for was the easy way out and making it a sexual crime only was used to build up public pressure and distort the fact.

The fact that a body is nude doesn’t mean that it was molested. Sometimes it’s done just to hide the identification."

John Wayne Gacy

"You know, if I wanted to kill somebody, I'd take this book and beat you to death with it and I wouldn't feel a thing. It'd be just like walking to the drug store."

Charles Manson

"Just random, senseless destruction."

Sam Dieteman

"There was a man, he was begging and pleading, and praying I guess. He was 'Please God'-ing all over the place. So I told him he could have a half hour to pray to God, and if God could come down and change the circumstances, he'd have that time.

But God never showed up and he never changed the circumstances, and that was that. It wasn't too nice. That's one thing I shouldn't have done, that one. I shouldn't have done it that way."

Richard Kuklinski

"I like children. They are tasty."

Albert Fish

"I opened her breast and with a knife and cut through the fleshy parts of the body. Then I arranged the body as a butcher does beef and hacked it with the axe into pieces.

I may say that while opening the body, I was so greedy that I trembled and could have cut out a piece and eaten it."

Andreas Bichel

"One side of me says, I'd like to talk to her, date her.

The other side of me says, I wonder what her head would look like on a stick?"

Edmund Kemper

"The women I killed were filth-bastard prostitutes who were littering the streets.

I was just cleaning up the place a bit."

Peter Sutcliffe

"The more I looked at people, the more I hated them."

Chalres Starkweather

"I have got to say this, it felt really, really, really good. One of the best things I have done in my life. "

Daniel Gonzalez

"The demons wanted my penis."

David Berkowitz

"In the morning he was lying dead on one of the beds fully clothed. He was dead. I got the impression he wanted to go, and I must have killed him.

I can't remember strangling him. I just sat there shocked."

Dennis Nilsen

"When I used my knife, it brought psychological relief. I know I have to be destroyed. I was a mistake of nature."

Andrei Chikatilo

"I sat down to think things over a bit. While I was sitting there, a little kid about eleven or twelve years old came bumming around. He was looking for something. He found it too.

I took him out to a gravel pit about one quarter miles away. I left him there, but first committed sodomy on him and then killed him.

His brains were coming out of his ears when I left him, and he will never be any deader."

Carl Panzram

"If you're going to do something, do it well, and leave something witchy"

Charles Manson

"I am rather unhappy because you people will not wear some nice Zodiac buttons. So I now have a little list, starting with the woman and her baby that I gave an interesting ride for a couple hours one evening a few months back that ended in my burning her car where I found them."

The Zodiac Killer

"I'm not interested in what the public thinks. My fight is in the courts. And while I have been fighting with the appeal it has been an uphill battle because I am an unpopular cause. Too much public pressure, too much politics.

To give me a hearing so that I can prove that the state withheld evidence favourable to me, that the identifications of some of the victims was wrong, and that my attorney was more concerned about book rights and how sensationally more the case could get, the higher the value of the book."

John Wayne Gacy

"What is done is done. If I leave here in ten, fifteen, twenty years, I'll go back to doing the same thing."

Pedro Rodrigues Filho

"Mostly I did it for the thrill of it."

Bobby Joe Long

"People like me don't come from films. Them films come from people like me."

David Harker

"A possessed dog in the neighborhood won't let me stop killing until he gets his fill of blood."

David Berkowitz

"I would cook it and look at the pictures and masturbate."

Jeffery Dahmer

"It was like a nightmare, I was in a movie."

Jeremy Bryan Jones

"The reason people piss me off is to test my trigger finger, & my adrenaline"

Eric Harris

"Even psychopaths have emotions, then again, maybe not."

Richard Ramirez

"There is much I'd like to say, Your Honor, about our world and my beliefs. However, I feel whatever I might have to say is overshadowed by the suffering I've caused. I regret with all my heart what my hand has done. I have taken what I cannot return.

If only I could bend back the hands of that ageless clock and change the past. Ah, but alas, I am not the keeper of time, only a small part of history and the legacy of man's fall from grace. I'm sorry, Your Honor. "

Danny Rolling

"Hurry it up, I could hang a dozen men while you're fooling around."

Carl Panzram

"I've killed no one. I've ordered no one to be killed. These children who come to you with their knives, they're your children. I didn't teach them, you did."

Charles Manson

"When I was a young man I found out that if you hurt somebody, they'll leave you alone. Good guys do finish last."

Richard Kuklinski

"I wish I could stop but I could not. I had no other thrill or happiness. "

Dennis Nilsen

"I've had photos of 21 of the victims and I've looked at them all over the years here and I've never recognized any one of them."

John Wayne Gacy

"They smelled bad."

Ed Gein

"I'd like to choose my own kind of death for a change.
I'm tired of being tormented to hell."

Jim Jones

"Gonna kill you. Bitch. Fucking whore."

Joseph James DeAngelo

"Twenty trained police officers came to the house with a warrant, searched the house, and they went down in the crawlspace while I was being held at the jail in Des Plaines, Illinois.

They never took anything from the crawlspace other than bringing up lime into the house. There also were no mounds of dirt like what is mentioned in books."

John Wayne Gacy

"Sex is one of my downfalls. I get sex any way I can get it. If I have to force somebody to do it, I do. I rape them. I've done that.

I've killed animals to have sex with them, and I've had sex while they're alive. "

Henry Lee Lucas

Most treasured hononr: “My dick.”
Perfect man or woman: “Me.”
Childhood hero: “Jack the Ripper”
Favorite TV show: “The Munsters”
Hobbies: “Slicing and dicing and spicing up rump roast.”
Favorite meals: “Women's feet.”
Ideal evening: “Full moon, sex and drugs all night.”
My biggest regret: “Not carrying a gun at all times. Ha.”

Richard Ramirez

"In this hole lives the wicked king."

David Berkowitz

"I wanted to be a soldier. I loved everything related to the military."

Mareel Barbeault

"I think in some way I wanted it to end, even if it meant my own destruction."

Jeffery Dahmer

"I have an obsession with the unattainable. I have to eliminate what I cannot attain."

Robert Bardo

"My first murder was thrilling because I had embarked on the career I had chosen for myself, the career of murder."

John Reginald Halliday Christie

"There is a devil sitting inside me which controls everything."

Anatoly Onoprienko

"They wouldn't be stereotypes necessarily. But they would be reasonable facsimiles to women as a class. A class not of women, per se, but a class that has almost been created through the mythology of women and how they are used as objects."

Ted Bundy

"I wasn't going to rob her or touch her or rape her.
I was just going to kill her."

David Berkowitz

"I don't believe in man, God, nor Devil. I hate the whole damned human race, including myself. I preyed upon the weak, the harmless and the unsuspecting. This lesson I was taught by others. Might makes right."

Carl Panzram

"Look down on me and you see a fool. Look up at me and you see a god. Look straight at me and you see yourself."

Charles Manson

"Possessing them physically as one would possess a potted plant, a painting, or a Porsche. Owning, as it were, this individual."

Ted Bundy

"All of the sudden I realized that I had just done something that separated me from the human race and it was something that could never be undone, I realized that from that point on I could never be like normal people.

I must have stood there in that state for 20 minutes. I have never felt an emptiness of self like I did right then and I never will forget that feeling. It was like I crossed over into a realm I could never come back from."

David Gore

"Killing became the same thing as having sex."

Henry Lee Lucas

"I would have liked to had a better outlook on life, but I can't change yesterday."

Richard Kuklinski

"I'm so happy, because my time is short here.
If you come with us your time can be shortened."

Marshall Applewhite

"I killed so many women I have a hard time keeping them straight."

Gary Ridgeway (Green River Killer)

"I don't remember killing anyone, I could have done it without knowing it. I am not sure if I did it."

Kenneth Erskine

"It is none of my concern.
I have no desire to be a part of society.
Society is not my concern."

Yang Xahai

"I want to master life and death."

Ted Bundy

"People are like maggots, small, blind and worthless."

David Smith

"It wasn't in the states best interest to let the jury know, they said it would raise doubt that John Gacy acted alone. The defense attorneys didn't bring it out because it didn't have it didn't go along with their insanity defense, showing others were involved."

John Wayne Gacy

"I saw him at peace in my armchair. I remember wishing he could stay in peace like that forever. I had a feeling of easing his burden with my strength."

Dennis Nilsen

"Take your worst nightmares and put my face to them."

Tommy Lynn Sells

"You will serve the Earth as much as she serves you or you will commit suicide."

Lynette "Squeaky" Fromme

"I will in all probability be convicted, but I will not go away as a monster, but as a tragedy."

Joel Rifkin

"Although my parents were kind and loving, I had none of the joys or the companionship which small children usually have. From my earliest years my recollection is of my father saying: 'Do no' or 'Thou shall not'.

Any form of sport or light entertainment was frowned upon and regarded as not edifying. There was only condemnation and prohibition."

John Haigh

“I had a compulsion to do it.”
Ed Gein

"We've all got the power in our hands to kill, but most people are afraid to use it. The ones who aren't afraid, control life itself."

Richard Ramirez

"If you spit in my face and smack me in the mouth and throw me into solitary confinement for nothing, what do you think's gonna happen when I get out of here?"

Charles Manson

"That is what has been said in the media and at the trial. To this day nobody has produced one. There is no written confession, there is no tape recorded confession, there is no police stenographer typed confession.

It was in my appeal and the court refused to look at it and the state refused to answer it. If they had nothing to hide I can't understand why they can't produce one."

John Wayne Gacy

“She isn't missing. She's at the farm right now.”

Ed Gein

"I have a lawyer."

Joseph James DeAngelo

"I'm the most cold-blooded sonofabitch you'll ever meet."

Ted Bundy

"I certainly wanted for my mother a nice, quiet, easy death like everyone else wants."

Edmund Kemper

"I didn't want to hurt them, I only wanted to kill them."

David Berkowitz

"My life don't make a lot of sense. It don't make sense that I go around the country killing people. Period. It don't make sense doing that."

Tommy Lynn Sells

"To my knowledge anybody that I've ever had sex with, male or female, are still alive. Any sex that I had was with consenting males or females."

John Wayne Gacy

"If I think about it, it would wind up hurting me, so I don't. I don't think about it."

Richard Kuklinski

"When this monster entered my brain I will never know, but it is here to stay. How does one cure himself? I can't stop it. The monster goes on and hurts me as well as society. Maybe you can stop him. I can't."

Dennis Rader (BTK)

"I'm a murderer, not a rapist."

Gary Ridgeway (Green River Killer)

“I am a robot. I don't feel anything.”

Anatoly Onoprienko

"I choked her to death, then cut her in small pieces so I could take my meat to my rooms, cook and eat it. How sweet and tender her little ass was roasted in the oven.

It took me 9 days to eat her entire body.

I did not fuck her, though."

Albert Fish

"I can't stand a bitchy chick."

Gerald Stano

"Sometimes I feel like a vampire."

Ted Bundy

"I made my fantasy life more powerful than my real one."

Jeffery Dahmer

"I was literally singing to myself on my way home after the killing. The tension, the desire to kill a woman had built up in such explosive proportions that when I finally pulled the trigger, all the pressures, all the tensions, all the hatred, had just vanished, dissipated, but only for a short time."

David Berkowitz

"For me a corpse has a beauty and dignity which a living body could never hold. There is a peace about death that soothes me."

John Reginald Halliday Christie

"I am the Devil and I'm here to do the Devil's business."

Charles "Tex" Watson

“A lot of people are tired around here, but I'm not sure they're ready to lie down, stretch out and fall asleep.”

Jim Jones

"I have several children who I'm turning into killers.
Wait till they grow up."

David Berkowitz

"I remember there was actually a sexual thrill. You hear that little pop and pull their heads off and hold their heads up by the hair. Whipping their heads off, their body sitting there. That'd get me off."

Edmund Kemper

"I am currently watching Dexter, the series about that forensic mass murderer"

Anders Breivik

"The fantasy that accompanies and generates the anticipation that precedes the crime is always more stimulating than the immediate aftermath of the crime itself."

Ted Bundy

"The smell of fresh blood, the bloody lumps, all this fascinated me."

Eusebius Pieydagnelle

"I rape and murder."

Luis Garavito

“I killed some tramps. I killed them because of you.”

Asghar the Murderer

"I like hurting people."

Daniel Camargo Barbosa

"Since this girl in front of him represented not a person, but again the image, or something desirable, the last thing we would expect him to want to do would be to personalize this person. Chattering and flattering and entertaining, as if seen through a motion picture screen."

Ted Bundy

"(Old people) should all be gassed."

Orville Lynn Majors

"Total paranoia is just total awareness."

Charles Manson

"I turn children into killers."

David Berkowitz

"Because my trial attorney's never did their job to investigate my claim, and it wasn't until we took over the investigation on my own that we learned of this. Even the F.B.I. joined in, in 1984 with their reasoning being that they wanted to know if others in other states disappeared or were murdered while I was in those states.

The results shows that during the time of the victims disappearances in Chicago. I wasn't even in Chicago. One judge said, so what if he was out of town for 16 of them, there are still 17 others. That alone should have raised some doubt."

John Wayne Gacy

"Killing prostitutes had become an obsession with me.
I could not stop myself. It was like a drug."

Peter Sutcliffe

"People do die suddenly of old age. They just wear out."

Harold Shipman

The people and the news media used to call me 'The Son of Sam,' but God has given me a new name, 'The Son of Hope,' because now my life is about hope."

David Berkowitz

"I haven't blocked out the past. I wouldn't trade the person I am, or what I've done, or the people I've known for anything. So I do think about it. And at times it's a rather mellow trip to lay back and remember."

Ted Bundy

"It was a sawed off shotgun. When it happened it surprised me. I expected the man to die but it really surprised me when it took his head off. It was something I didn't expect."

Richard Kuklinski

"Keep in mind the public has been brainwashed and nearly 80% of what is known about me is fantasy and self serving theories of the state. But overall, I am an embarrassment of the justice system because if I am right then they are wrong and the killers are still out there.

For political reasons it would be better that I drop dead, then they could all say what a great job they've done and nobody else would be pushing for the truth to come out."

John Wayne Gacy

"With a girl, there's a lot left in the girl's body without a head. Of course, the personality is gone."

Edmund Kemper

"I am a monster. I am the Son of Sam. I love to hunt."

David Berkowitz

"As I grew up I realized, though imperfectly, that I was different from other people, and that the way of life in my home was different from that in the homes of others....This stimulated me to introspection and strange mental questionings."

John Haigh

"It's not so much that I want to (die), but if that's what the people want, I'm not going to waste a bunch of time and fight..."

Sam Dieteman

"Yes I marked the spot in the garage when I was back at the house on December 22. They had asked me with all of the rebuilding of the garage, which was the last area of concrete, in the last area where the concrete was poured. And they handed me an orange spray can and I put an ‘X’. That’s it.

An ‘X’ over the spot in the corner of the garage where I thought the last area was poured. Now all of a sudden Kunkle claims that I not only drew an ‘X’, but I put an ‘O’ on top of it where the head was and made the ‘X’ look like it was a stick figure, and that’s not true."

John Wayne Gacy

"A man's gotta make at least one bet a day, else he could be walking around lucky and never know it."

Jim Jones

"Chainsaws are messy... Why would I want to ruin a good shirt with a chainsaw? That would be downright stupid."

Richard Kuklinski

"Well, I guess you got me good. Yes, I killed them. All the ones in the paper. I did them all."

Bobby Joe Long

"This is no way to be.
Man ought to be free.
That man should be me."

Ted Bundy

"In the case of Ohliger, I also sucked blood from the wound on her temple, and from Scheer from the stab in the neck.

From the girl Schulte I only licked the blood from her hands. It was the same with the swan in the Hofgarten. I used to stroll at night through the Hofgarten very often, and in the spring of 1930 I noticed a swan sleeping at the edge of the lake.

I cut its throat. The blood spurted up and I drank from the stump and ejaculated."

Peter Kurten

"Big deal, death comes with the territory.
See you in Disneyland."

Richard Ramirez

DAVID PARKER RAY

THE TOYBOX KILLER

Audio Tape Transcription

The following is a transcript of the prerecorded cassette tape which American serial killer David Parker Ray played for his victims. It describes in graphic detail the ways in which they were tortured before death.

Although only 3 victims were confirmed, Ray is suspected of committing the atrocities described below on over sixty women throughout his reign of terror.

"Hello there, bitch. Are you comfortable right now? I doubt it. Wrists and ankles chained. Gagged. Probably blind folded. You are disoriented and scared, too, I would imagine. Perfectly normal, under the circumstances. For a little while, at least, you need to get your shit together and listen to this tape.

It is very relevant to your situation. I'm going to tell you, in detail, why you have been kidnapped, what's going to happen to you and how long you'll be here. I don't know the details of your capture, because this tape is being created July 23rd, 1993 as a general advisory tape for future female captives.

The information I'm going to give you is based on my experience dealing with captives over a period of several years. If, at a future date, there are any major changes in our procedures, the tape will be upgraded.

Now, you are obviously here against your will, totally helpless, don't know where you're at, don't know what's gonna happen to you. You're very scared or very pissed off. I'm sure that you've already tried to get your wrists and ankles loose, and know you can't. Now you're just waiting to see what's gonna happen next.

You probably think you're gonna be raped and you're fuckin' sure right about that. Our primary interest is in what you've got between your legs. You'll be raped thoroughly and repeatedly, in every hole you've got.

Any time that we go on a hunting trip, if we can't find a little teenager, we usually start hittin' the gay bars, look for a well-built, big-titted lesbian. I thoroughly enjoy rapin' and screwin' around with lesbians, and there's not as much danger of them carrying a sexually transmitted disease. And I don't like usin' condoms. Also, even though they're a little older, unless they've been playing with dildos a lot, they still have tight holes between their legs, like the younger girls.

If we can't find a lesbian that we want, we snatch anything that is young, clean and well built. We very seldom come back empty handed, cause there's plenty of bitches out there to choose from. And, with a little practice in deception, most of em' is very easy to get, with little risk. At this point, it makes little difference what category you fall into.

You're here and we're gonna make the most of it. You're going to be kept in a hidden slave room. It is relatively sound proof, escape proof, and it is completely stocked with devices and equipment to satisfy our sexual fetishes and deviations. There may or may not be another girl in the room. Occasionally, for variety, we like to keep two slaves at the same time. In either case, as the new girl, you'll definitely be getting the most attention for a while. Now, as I said earlier, you're going to be kept like an animal. I guess I been doin' this too long.

I've been rapin' bitches ever since I was old enough to jerk off, and tie little girls' hands behind their back. As far as I'm concerned, you're a pretty piece of meat, to be used and exploited.

I don't give a flyin' fuck about your mind or how you feel about this situation. You may be married, have a kid or two, boyfriend, girlfriend, a job, car payment. Fuck it. I don't give a rat's ass about any of that, and I don't want to hear about it. It's something you're gonna have to deal with after you're turned loose.

I make it a point never to like a slave and I fuckin' sure don't have any respect for you. Here, your status is no more than that of one of the dogs, or of one of the animals out in the barn. Your only value to us is the fact that you have an attractive, usable body. And, like the rest of our animals, you will be fed and watered, kept in good physical condition, kept reasonably clean and allowed to use the toilet when necessary. In return, you're gonna be used hard, especially during your first few days while you're new and fresh.

You're gonna be kept chained in a variety of different positions, usually with your legs or knees forced wide apart.

Your pussy and asshole is gonna get a real workout. Especially your asshole, because I'm into animal sex. Also, both of those holes are going to be subjected to a lotta use with some rather large dildos, among other things. And it goes without sayin', that there's gonna be a lot of oral sex. On numerous occasions, you're gonna be forced to suck cock and eat pussy until your jaws ache and your tongue is sore. You may not like it, but you're fuckin' sure gonna do it. And that's the easy part.

Our fetishes and hang-ups include stringent bondage, dungeon games, a little sadism, nothing serious but uncomfortable and sometimes painful. Just a few little hang-ups that we like to use when we're gettin' off on a bitch. Heh, heh. If you're a young teeny bopper, and ignorant about fetishes and deviations, you're about to get an enlightening crash course in sex. Who knows, you may like some of it. It happens, occasionally. If we wanna take the time and trouble, even under these conditions, most bitches can be brought to orgasm.

Now I've already told you that you're gonna be here a month or two, or maybe three, if you keep us turned on. If it's up to my lady, we'd keep you indefinitely. She says it's just as much fun and less risky. But personally, I like variety. A fresh pussy, now and then, to play with. We take four or five different girls each year, depending on our urges and sometimes accidental encounters.

Basically, I guess we are like predators. We're always lookin'. Occasionally, some sweet little thing will be broke down on the side of the road, walkin', bicyclin', joggin'. Anytime an opportunity like that presents itself, and it's not too risky, we'll grab her. Even if we've already got a captive in the playroom. Variety is definitely the spice of life.

Now I'm sure that you're a great little piece of ass and you're gonna be a lot of fun to play with, but I will get tired of you eventually. If I killed every bitch that we kidnapped, there'd be bodies strung all over the country. And besides, I don't like killin' a girl, unless it is absolutely necessary.

So I've devised a safe, alternate method of disposal. I had plenty of bitches to practice on over the years, so I've pretty well got it down pat. And I enjoy doin' it. I get off on mind games.

After we get completely through with you, you're gonna be drugged up real heavy, with a combination of Sodium Pentothal and Phenobarbital. They are both hypnotic drugs that will make you extremely susceptible to hypnosis, autohypnosis and hypnotic suggestion. You're gonna be kept drugged a couple of days, while I play with your mind. By the time I get through brainwashing you, you're not gonna remember a fuckin' thing about this little adventure. You won't remember this place, us, or what has happened to you. There won't be any DNA evidence, because you'll be bathed, and both holes between your legs will be thoroughly flushed out.

You'll be dressed, sedated, and turned loose on some country road, bruised, heh, sore all over, but nothing that won't heal up in a week or two. The thought of being brainwashed may not be appealing to you, but we been doin' it a long time and it works. And it's the lesser of two evils. I'm sure that you would prefer that, in lieu of being strangled or having your throat cut.

Okay, undoubtedly, somebody's gonna be lookin' for you. There may or may not be a missing persons report. But nobody's gonna be lookin' for you here. They don't have any idea where you're at. You don't even know where you're at. We're always very careful about that.

There are not gonna be any knights in shining armor coming to rescue you. You are strictly on your own and, under the circumstances, I bet that is a scary thought. If there is another girl in the room, she won't be able to help you either. Because she's gonna be in the same position you're in. As for escaping, I'm sure you'll try to figure out a way. That's human nature. But it's not hardly even worth talking about here.

It would not be prudent on our part to have you running around in the woods screamin' rape. It would be an embarrassment, to say the least. Consequently, you are gonna be kept in an environment that is even more secure than a prison cell. If it has not already been done, very shortly a steel collar is going to be padlocked around your neck. It has a long, heavy chain that is padlocked to a ring in the floor. The collar will never be removed, until you are turned loose. It's a permanent fixture.

The hidden playroom, where you're gonna be kept, has steel walls, floor and ceiling. It is virtually soundproof and has a steel door with two keyed locks. The hinges are welded on and there are two heavy deadbolts on the outside. The room is totally escape proof, even with tools.

Any time that you are left unattended in the room, your wrists will be chained and there are electronic sensors to, uh, let us know if you move around too much. And if that's not enough, there is a closed-circuit TV system with a surveillance camera. It's wired to the main TV in the living room so we can check you once in awhile, or just set and watch you for the fun of it.

Electronics is a wonderful thing. Expensive, but hell, everything in the room is expensive, and damn well worth it. If everybody knew how much fun it was to keep a sex slave, half the women would be chained up in somebody's basement.

Anyway, we've had a lot of practice at this and, uh, we're not real concerned about you escaping. You're fuckin' sure not gonna go anywhere. Now if you're not already naked, you soon will be. Your clothing will be bagged up and saved until such time as we decide to turn you loose. As far as being naked goes, you might as well get used to it. For what you are gonna be used for, clothing would just be in the way. Besides, I like watching a naked woman's body, all of it, whether it be in a room or on the TV set.

As I've already said, you'll be fed and watered on a regular basis. Not as much of either as you're used to, I'm sure, but enough to keep you healthy. You'll only be fed once a day, like the rest of the animals. And during the first few days, until you adjust to it and your stomach shrinks up, you're going to feel a little weak and you'll be hungry all the time. It won't take long, three or four days. And during the first few days, until you adjust to the environment, I prefer to keep you in a weakened condition anyway.

Now you already know that you've been kidnapped and brought here for us to train and use as a sex slave. I realize that being abducted and being forced into sexual slavery is a hard pill to swallow.

Some girls really have a lot of trouble with it and I'm sure that you will, to a certain extent. But face it, you can't get away, you can't say no. You're gonna be naked all the time. You won't be able to struggle or resist. You're gonna have to lay there and take it, good or bad, no matter what is being done to you. A scary thought? Yes, but there are no options. Nothing that you can say or do will change the fact that it's going to happen.

Many girls beg and plead. Almost all of 'em cry a lot, especially during the first three or four days. And some of 'em scream and threaten. But I have a poster on the wall in the playroom that says it all. If they're worth takin', they're worth keepin'. And I'm going to tell you, just so you know, since you are being kept here against your will, we will never trust anything you say, do or promise.

You are a potential threat to us and you will always be treated as such. On numerous occasions, bitches have told me that they'd do anything I wanted 'em to do, if I'd just take the chains off. I've been offered ransom money and I've even had girls tell me they liked it. But I like to use the chains, money's not that important and masochists are rare as hell. Heh, heh, I wonder what your scam's gonna be. Not anything that I haven't heard before, I bet, if you get a chance to talk at all.

Well, let's change the subject, a little bit. You already know that, for the most part, you're gonna be kept in the playroom. But, once in awhile, we like to take a captive into the bedroom, in chains of course.

Also, we have a couple of real close friends that we party with once in awhile. They know about our hang-ups and don't have any problem with fuckin' a slave. You may be required to service them occasionally. But that's an easy one, for the most part, just fuckin' and suckin'. They don't get into the heavier stuff.

However, when we have a party, sometimes I like to put on a little show that you won't like at all. You'll be taken into the living room and put on the floor on your hands and knees, naked. Your wrists, ankles, knees and hips will be strapped to a metal frame to hold your body in that position. The frame is designed for doggie fuckin', your ass up in the air, sex organs exposed, your tits hangin' down on each side of a metal support bar, knees spread about twelve inches, position similar to that of a bitch dog in heat, right in the middle of the floor so we can set on the couch and in chairs, and watch.

I'm going to rub canine breeder's musk on your back, the back of your neck, and on your sex organs. Now I have three dogs. All of 'em's male, cause I don't need any fuckin' pups. One of 'em is a very large German shepherd that is always horny, and he loves it when I bring him in the house to fuck a woman.

After I let him in the house, he'll sniff around you a little bit and, within a minute, he'll be mounting you. There's about a 50–50 chance which hole he'll get his penis into, but it doesn't seem to bother him whether it's the pussy or the asshole. His penis is pretty thin.

It goes in easy, but it's about ten inches long and when he gets completely excited, it gets a hell of a knot right in the middle of it.

Now I've had slaves tell me that it feels like they got a baseball inside of 'em. It doesn't take long. He's gonna hump you real fast for about three or four minutes. And while he's doin' it, he'll wrap his front legs around your chest to hold himself in position. And, in the process, he'll probably scratch your tits up a little bit, with his claws. After he gets through, he usually turns around and tries to pull out. Oh, he'll jerk a little, not much, mostly just steady pressure. And I've timed it.

The knot will usually shrink up enough to come outta your pussy in about three minutes. If he's in your asshole, about five minutes. I don't use the dog all that often, but I don't deprive him of pussy either. There's no doubt that he's going to be on you a few times while you're here, because I like watching it. And any time it's just you, me and the dog, it will always be in your butt.

The dog knot on his penis is big and extremely uncomfortable when he's, uh, pushing it back and forth way up in her anus. I really enjoy watching a girl wiggle, jerk and squirm around while he's doing it. Consequently, I give him a little, uh, assistance getting it in the right hole.

Now if you think all of this stuff is sick and depraved, you haven't seen anything yet.

This is a different world. Among our small circle of friends, little things like rape, kidnapping, doggie fucking, stuff like that, are every-day occurrences. Matter of course. Here, anything can happen and often does. We like livin' in the mountains, because it's quiet, secluded, private and everybody minds their own business. The only close house belongs to our friends and they don't hear or see anything.

Okay, let's talk about, uh, your training, the rules and punishment. Here, you are a slave and discipline is extremely strict. You're gonna be given a set of rules, things you can and cannot do, and you will learn to comply because each time you violate a rule, you will be punished. As soon as each rule is told to you, it will become law as far as you're concerned. And you know what's gonna happen every time you fuck up. We'll use a couple of methods of punishment.

A whip is an excellent training aid, so is an electro shock machine. Any time you get out of line, one or both will be used on your body and I assure you, it will not be pleasant. There is not many rules and they're very easy to remember. But you're gonna make mistakes. Every slave does. I don't like repeat offenders.

It gets me very upset. During the first few hours, the first time you violate a certain rule [tape recording skips here] a teaching process. The second time you violate the same rule, you'll be lightly punished. And the third time you violate it, it's gonna be full punishment.

After the first day, we won't cut you any slack at all. We will expect total obedience. Now let's start this off right. You are a slave. You don't realize it yet, but you will eventually. I'm your master and the lady is your mistress. You will be totally docile. You'll be very quiet and you'll speak only when spoken to. Never initiate conversation. Keep your mouth shut. Any time that you are spoken to, you will be required to respond and it will be with proper speech.

Remember that we are in the dungeon game and as long as you are here, it's the only game in town. Any time that you are asked a question where a yes or no answer is required, you will respond by saying, "yes, master; no,mistress; no, master; etcetera."

You will show proper respect. Having to use the word master or mistress may sound funny, petty or vain to you, but that's all right. If you choose not to do it, you can laugh while you're being whipped or when your body is convulsing under the electroshock machine. You will respond to commands without protest or resistance. Do exactly what you're told, nothing else. Remember that here you are a slave and failure to respond to a command will definitely get you in trouble. If I decide to rape you in your pussy or in your asshole, don't resist or struggle.

When I tell you to spread your legs, or to pull em back, you say, "yes, master" and obey the command, cause to do anything less will get you beaten. If I tell you I want to be sucked off, you say, "yes, master" and open your mouth. I love oral sex, if it's done right. You're going to be taught exactly the way I like it.

How to use your lips and tongue. We'll be practicing a lot and each time, when I get ready to come, I'm going to push my penis down your throat and keep it there until I get through squirtin'. I'm not gonna choke you, but you need to learn to hold your breath and to swallow every bit of the sperm. If I see one drop leaking out of your mouth, I'm gonna punish you. Basically, it's gonna be the same with your mistress. If she demands oral sex, you say yes mistress and respond.

She also will teach you exactly the way she likes it. And you will keep using your tongue on her pussy until she gets off. Now, I can't foresee what kind of bitch you're gonna be, how you feel about oral sex or any of that shit. But I am gonna tell you this. If, during oral sex or any other time, you should bite one of us, I'm going to cut on you a little bit. I'll cut your nipple off for a starter and if it's a bad bite, I'll cut your tit off, too.

That may sound harsh, but your teeth are serious weapons and we're not gonna tolerate any shit from you. I have been bitten and I've cut off nipples, so don't fuck around. That's enough said about that. Remember the commands, yes, master; no, mistress.

If your mistress should come into the room and tells you to get down on the floor or lay down on the floor, you say, "yes, mistress" and then lay down on the floor exactly the way she told you to do. If she tells you to pull your knees up, you say, "yes, mistress" and pull your knees up.

If she tells you to spread your knees, you say, "yes, mistress" and spread 'em, wide apart and hold them there so she can play with your pussy, use dildos or whatever.

A slave must always obey every command and offer no resistance. Remember that. Never say no unless it's justified, like in response to a question. If either one, or both of us, decide to put you in a different bondage position, the chains will be taken off the various parts of your body, wrists and ankles, never off of your neck.

Don't kick, struggle or resist in any way. If you do, you're going to be in a world of hurt. If you're told to hold your leg out so a chain can be attached to your ankle, you say, "yes, master" or "yes, mistress," and hold your leg out. For repeated rule violations, the punishments are eventually gonna become harsh and even brutal and you won't have anyone to blame but yourself.

Now I should also tell you that there's gonna be times when the whip and electroshock is used not for punishment, but for our pleasure. The difference will be that when it's done for pleasure, the whip strokes will be much lighter. They'll sting like hell, but they won't have that burning sensation and leave welts that hurt for hours.

As for the electroshock machine, the voltage will be turned down. It won't be that harsh electricity that, uh, makes your body convulse and jerk all over the table. You haven't experienced any of that yet, but I'm sure that you will.

To avoid these punishments you're gonna have to be very quiet, very docile, and very obedient and I imagine that's gonna be very hard for you to do.

You'll probably try us a few times, to see if this is real. Heh, heh, most captives do. If you want to, be my guest, because it's all part of the game. Now let's discuss talking. You cannot talk, you cannot speak unless you've been given permission. I believe that rule gets more bitches in trouble than anything else, because they can't keep their damn mouth shut. They always wanna whine, beg, plead, try to talk me into turning 'em loose. I used to listen to it. I don't anymore. I enjoy blessed silence. Around here, your mouth is for sucking, not talking.

Around here, the only time I ever want to hear you initiate speech is if you have to use the restroom, and you will learn to do it properly. Master, may I please use the restroom, or mistress, may I please use the restroom. In response, we will ask you what you need to do. If you have to pee, you say, "pee,master" or "pee, mistress." If you have to crap, you say,"crap, master," or "crap, mistress."

It will be done that way because, quite often, you will be in heavy restraints, a lot of straps on your body, chains on your wrists and ankles, a bunch of stuff that's, uh, time consuming and hard to get loose. If you have to pee, we'll use a bed pan.

If you have to shit, you may have to hold it awhile. Whatever the case, we need to know. And you definitely need to tell us. Because if you make a mess, you're going to be punished and you have to clean it up. Now, I've covered the basics pretty thoroughly. You know to keep your mouth shut and not try to talk. You know the proper way to say master or mistress and you know how you're expected to act and respond to commands. If you can learn to do all of that, there will not be a great deal of punishment. We'll get along pretty good.

There's going to be a lot of other things done to your body besides just fuckin' and suckin'. But for that, for the most part, you'll either be in stringent bondage, or strapped down on a gynecology table. You won't be able to struggle or resist anyway. Now you're going to be required to learn fast. Training is not one of my favorite things to do and I prefer fucking around with a slave that's already trained.

I've already given you the basics, so there is not that much to learn. But until you accept the fact that you are a slave, you're gonna have problems with it. Remember that each time you fuck up, you are gonna be punished. And after it's happened a few times, you're really gonna dread it. Some girls tend to be a little rebellious. I sure as hell wouldn't advise that, cause it will get you in serious trouble.

Here, you definitely need to be docile. You're not in any position to be otherwise. We've done this so many times that we know exactly what we like to do with a slave.

We don't go out of our way to brutalize a girl. If you don't give us any trouble, we won't do any more to your body than is necessary to satisfy our sexual needs. Initially, when we've got a new girl in the playroom, we're kinda like a kid with a new toy.

You are fresh and exciting and we're gonna spend a lot of time playing with you. Later, after the newness wears off, things will settle into something of a routine. We'll only be spending three or four hours each day in the playroom. You're gonna have a lot of free time to rest, sleep, watch TV, or whatever. If you're acting halfway decent, you'll be left in a reasonably comfortable position so you can relax.

As far as sex goes, your mistress is going to want her pussy eaten a couple of times a day. For my part, I like getting' off in a slave twice and sometimes three times each day, usually in her mouth or in her asshole. Don't get me wrong. I'm gonna be stickin' my dick in your cunt once in awhile, too. But for the most part when I use that hole, it's going to be with, uh, large dildos.

We're going to be in and out of the room several times each day, but you will have a lot of free time. Now I gotta tell you that there's another side to the coin. Once in awhile we get a bitch that is resentful, rebellious, won't mind, uncooperative. That doesn't work here. I'm sure that you realize you're on thin ice. As long as you have chains on your body, don't try either one of us. It is an extremely dangerous thing to do because, if necessary, I'm capable of doing things to your body and torturing you in ways that you can't even imagine.

The playroom is equipped with a full set of surgical instruments which I have had occasion to use and will again, as necessary. I've already told you what'll happen if you bite. To be completely safe here, you have to be docile.

If you should accidentally, or otherwise, hurt, scratch or kick either one of us, you could be in very serious trouble. I'm sure that you want to survive this experience, and I want you to also. But you are expendable and it's no big deal to go out and snatch a replacement. It may sound harsh and cold, but if you give us too much trouble, or if you pose any kind of a threat to us, I won't have any qualms at all about slicing your throat.

Like I said before, I don't like killin' the girls that we bring here, but occasionally things happen. What can I say? I would really hate to have to dump that pretty little body off in a canyon somewhere to rot. I'm not trying to scare you. That's just the way it is.

Be nice. Keep your mouth shut, learn the rules and survive. We are into S&M and you're going to be hurt a little, but everything we do to a girl is designed to cause pain, not injury. There is a big difference. No matter how painful it is, nothing that we plan to do to your body will cause any serious or permanent damage. I'm not lying to you or trying to make it sound easier, because that would be pointless. I'm just telling it like it is. That's the way we do things and that's the way it's gonna be, unless we have problems with you. I've already told you that you're gonna be whipped lightly, for pleasure. The electroshock will be used lightly, for pleasure.

Most of the other nasty little things that we're going to do, for the most part, will be done on your breasts, nipples and between your legs. The lady is fortunate. She can get off any time. She just likes to be a little sadistic with a slave once in awhile. In my case, I cannot get off with a girl unless I hurt her first. That's basically the reason I'm into rape and slavery, and the reason that you're going to be subjected to acertain amount of pain.

Mostly what we do to a captive is stick needles in her breasts and through her nipples, through her cunt lips, through her clit, and I'm into stretching certain things. Clamps, with long nylon cords on each one, will occasionally be put on your cunt lips so your pussy can be kept pulled open, and they're also going to be attached to your nipples. The nylon cords will be put through ceiling rings, or rings on each side of the table, and pulled very tight to stretch your tits.

Occasionally, your clit will also be clamped and stretched and we're gonna be using dildos. The dildos are gonna be used a lot, more than anything else, and consequently, what you're going to have the most trouble with. Many of them are long, very large in diameter and very painful while they're being forced in. Your mistress will use them in your pussy and I like to use them in both holes.

Actually, that pretty well covers it. There's gonna be a few other little things that we do. Nothing of any greater consequence and not often, just variety. As far as needles goes, they'll always be sterilized.

The clamps are gonna hurt like a motherfucker, but they won't cause any permanent injury. They don't even break the skin. As far as the dildos go, both of those holes between your legs will stretch a hell of a lot. It'll hurt, but they'll stretch. Your pussy is designed for a baby to come out of and we won't be using anything bigger than that. The really large ones will not be used in your butt. I don't wanna stretch that hole so big that it's not usable for fucking.

Anyway, that pretty well covers that part of it. Let's see, what have I missed? Let's talk about screaming. Every once in awhile we get a screamer. Some bitch that just wants to scream all the time. And it definitely gets 'em in trouble, because it gets on my nerves. Very shortly, that gag is going to be removed. We live in an isolated area, so screaming is not usually a problem. In the playroom it's not much of a problem at all because of the soundproofing. But it irritates the fuck out of me.

There is a time and a place. Occasionally I like to hear a bitch scream, but usually not. The only thing that screaming is gonna get you around here is a lot of punishment. And, if you do it habitually, I will just keep a ball gag in your mouth all the time. It'll only be taken out for you to eat and suck.

I've already told you about talking. Don't try to initiate a conversation. Don't say anything. You will be punished. If you're a smoker, now's a good time to quit. I'm not gonna buy your cigarettes and if you ask for one, the only thing you're gonna get is a few whip marks.

Remember, when you're asked a question, you say, "yes, master" or "no, master." If you have to go to the restroom, it is "master," or "mistress," may I please go to the restroom. Any time that you are given a command, always acknowledge the order verbally, "yes, master," and then obey the order. That's not too difficult.

A bright little thing like you should be able to learn it real fast. There are gonna be times when you are under a stress, a certain amount of stress and you may forget. But that's no excuse. Each time you fuck up, you are gonna be punished. After you're here a few days, it'll eventually become automatic and there'll no longer be a problem.

I realize that, after awhile, when I take that gag off, you are really gonna want to try to talk to me, talk me into turning you loose and such. It's because, with your wrists and ankles chained, your mouth is the only defense you have. But don't do it. It won't work and all it will bring is punishment.

Your first day here is not gonna be too difficult. There won't be any serious dungeon games. Your training has already been initiated, so you'll have to be very careful what you say and how you act. But for the most part, there's gonna be a little exploring. We will become very familiar with your body, and do a little fuckin' and suckin'. We may tease you a little bit with some of our more humane toys, but nothing serious. It's gonna be kind of an adjustment period. Don't say anything. Don't struggle or resist, no matter what we do, because we are going to start enforcing the rules immediately.

Now later, I'm gonna be asking you a bunch of questions. Since I'm gonna be caring for your body for the next month or two, or three, there are certain things that I need to know. I have prepared a questionnaire that I fill out with each new captive. Some of the questions are going to be embarrassing, but you should answer them truthfully and completely. You damn well better. I don't wanna catch you in a lie.

The questions will be in reference to your physical condition, any medical conditions that I'd need to know about, medications, sex habits, sexual preferences, any childbirth you mighta had, period dates and so forth.

Now your training has already started. Each time I ask you one of those questions on the questionnaire, there's gonna be a proper way to answer it, which I'll tell you about in a few minutes. While we go through the questionnaire, you're going to be strapped down on the gynecology table. Your feet will be in the stirrups and your knees will be pulled wide apart, with everything exposed. I like to keep a girl that way while she's answering the questions, so I can examine and verify, uh, anything she might tell me which would affect her use as a sex slave.

If you do have any kind of medical condition, by all means, let me know. We'll discuss it and we may make adjustments. We won't turn you loose, but we may make adjustments. We're probably going to be starting on this questionnaire pretty soon. You will be naked, and as I said, you'll be strapped down on a gynecology table so you can't wiggle or squirm around.

You will be talking quite a bit, answering the questions, so I'm sure that we'll start your speech training at the same time. Consequently, before we start on the questionnaire, two small electrical clamps will be put on your nipples. Each time a question is asked, you will respond properly. For instance, if I ask you how old you are, you will respond by saying, "Master, I'm nineteen years old."

Answer the question completely and say nothing else. If the question requires a yes or no answer, say, "Yes, master" or "No, master."

If I ask you your period dates, you say, "Master, my period is so and so."

If I ask you about childbirth, you say, "No, master," or "Master, I had a baby a year ago," or whatever.

Always start each sentence by saying "master." And take your time. We're not gonna be in any hurry. Think about what you're gonna say before you say it. Because each time you fuck up, I'm gonna press a little button and send a few thousand volts of electricity through your nipples, right down into your tits.

You are in training, so it will just be a quick blast. I'm not going to hold it down and torture you. But, each time you screw up, it's gonna be a little bit worse. So take your time. Answer the questions properly. I'm not gonna push you. We're not gonna be in any hurry. Think about each thing you're gonna say and be damn sure and start your sentence with master.

If you get through that okay, get your speech down pat, keep your mouth shut and don't give us any trouble, then the first day is gonna be real pleasant for everybody. I'm gonna put some dildos in those holes between your legs, but they will not be big ones.

Basically, I just wanna become very familiar with your sex organs and the size of the holes. All girls are different. During the course of the day, you're gonna be raped several times, but that's no big deal. The second day, after you get totally familiar with the rules and procedures, we're gonna get down to the nitty gritty.

A lot of it will not be very pleasant for you, but you might as well get used to it because it's gonna be like that for awhile. Eventually things will settle down a little. Then, just take it day by day. Well, I believe I've told you about everything that I can. I cannot predict the future. I can't predict changes of procedure. But if this tape is being played for you, I have to assume that it is still reasonably accurate. And I can only give you advice.

Be smart and be a survivor. Don't ever scream. Don't talk without permission. Be very quiet. Be docile and obedient and, by all means, show proper respect.

Have a nice day."

SEUNG HUI CHO

THE VIRGINIA TECH SHOOTER

Manifesto

The following is a manifesto sent by Seung Hui Cho to the news media on April 16, 2007, shortly before he murdered 32 people and wounded 17 others on the Virginia Tech college campus. Cho committed suicide before he could be arrested.

Cho was diagnosed with severe anxiety disorder with selective mutism and major depressive disorder.

Oh the happiness I could have had mingling among you hedonists, being counted as one of you, only if you didn't fuck the living shit out of me.

You could have been great. I could have been great. Ask yourself what you did to me to have made me clean the slate. Only if you could be the victim of your reprehensible and wicked crimes, you Christian Nazis, you would have brute-restrained your animal urges to fuck me.

You could be at home right now eating your fucking caviar and your fucking cognac, had you not ravenously raped my soul.

For every action, there is an equal and opposite reaction. Can you feel the pain that you fucked us in, you Descendants of Satan? Well, can you feel it? All the shit you've given me, right back at you with hollow points.

Don't you just wish you finished me off when you had the chance? Don't you just wish you killed me? You had a hundred billion chances and ways to have avoided today, but you decided to spill my blood.

You forced me into a corner and gave me only one option. The decision was yours. Now you have blood on your hands that will never wash off, you Apostles of Sin. Congratulations. You have succeeded in extinguishing my life. Vandalizing my heart wasn't enough for you. Raping my soul wasn't enough for you. Committing emotional sodomy on me wasn't enough for you.

Every single second wasted on your wanton hedonism and menacing sadism could have been used to prevent today. Ask yourselves, What was I doing all this time?

All these months, hours, seconds. Only if you could have been the victim of your crimes. Only if you could have been the victim. To you sadistic snobs, I may be nothing but a piece of dog shit.

You have vandalized my heart, raped my soul, and torched my conscious again and again. You thought it was one pathetic, void life that you were extinguishing.

Thanks to you, I die, like Jesus Christ, to inspire generations of the Weak and Defenseless people — my Brothers, Sisters, and Children — that you fuck. Like Moses, I spread the sea and lead my people — the Weak, the Defenseless, and the Innocent Children of all ages that you fucked and will always try to fuck — to eternal freedom.

Thanks to you Sinners, you Spillers of Blood, I set the example of the century for my Children to follow. You may stand steadfast on the battlefield of your life's dedication to eternal terrorism American Al-Qaeda, but the Children that you have fucked will rise. By the power greater than God we will hunt you down, you Lovers of Terrorism, and we will kill you.

Do they wanna fuck us and pretend to be devout Christians? Do they wanna smear dog shit on our face then give us a dirty towel to wipe away? Do they wanna rape us then give us stained toilet paper to clean up?

Do they wanna cut our throat then give us a used band aid to patch up? Do they wanna perpetrate endless sessions of crucifixions and holocausts on our innocent life then go to church and praise the Lord and Jesus? Do they wanna fuck us and pretend to be Jesus Christ?

I say we're the Jesus Christs, my Brothers, Sisters, and Children. Jesus Christ exists in us all: Ax Jesus Christ, John Jesus Christ, Jane Jesus Christ, Seung Jesus Christ, Carlos Jesus Christ, Hakeem Jesus Christ, Mohammad Jesus Christ, Zhang Jesus Christ, Oliver Jesus Christ, Elizabeth Jesus Christ, Vladimir Jesus Christ. Jesus Christ.

I say there is no pain they can inflict on us that they haven't already inflicted. I say they can't fuck us any more than they have already done. I say there are no lies they can say about us that they haven't already said. I say fuck you, you Descendants of Satan Disguised as Devout Christians.

I say we take up the cross, take up our guns and knives and hammers, and take no prisoners and spare no lives until our last breath and last ounce of energy. Seer of Veracity. Seal of the Anti-Terrorist. Number of the Anti-Terrorist.

You wanna rape us John Mark Karrs? You wanna rape us Debra LaFaves? Fuck you.

By destroying we create. We create the feelings in you of what it is like to be the victim, what it is like to be fucked and destroyed.

Because of your annihilations, we create and raise new breeds of Children who will show you fuckers what you have done to us.

Like Easter, it will be a day of rebirth. It will be a start of a revolution of the Children that you fucked. You have never felt a single ounce of pain your whole life, thus, by destroying you, by giving you pain, we attempt to show you responsibilities and meanings of other people's lives.

It's grand for you to fuck us 24/7 for fun, but we can't have a single minute of harmless playtime, only suffer. It's dandy for you to rape us, but we're not allowed to even speak, only be raped? Fuck you.

You love to pretend to, but you Hedonists, Charlatans, Sadists, Rapists, Terrorists will never know the feelings of giving up your lives for a cause. You have never felt a single ounce of pain in your hedonistic lives.

You will never give up a single can of your Bud Light, a shot of your cognac, or a half-drop of your own precious blood for another human being, only fuck the shit out of him and lie afterwards.

You fucked us, now we fuck you, now we kill you. There can be no lighter penalty for Masqueraded Democratic Terrorists who commit unforgivable acts of treason against mankind. There is no where in the world you can run, you Lovers of Terrorism.

There is nowhere in the world you can hide, you Lovers of Sadism. You will never know when and where the Weak and Defenseless that you fucked will strike — day, night, at school, in the public, in your home, during your most comfortable hour and protected place. You will never know how we will kill you — slash your throat, bullet in your back, torture you with knives, hammers, bolt cutters, scissors.

You will always live in fear. You will never be able to go to school or work or rest or sleep. Your heart will always pound nonstop. Your sin-ridden soul will slowly eat up your conscious for the heinous crimes you have committed.

So if you don't want to die a painful death, do yourself a favor, do yourself a coup de grace, and kill yourself clean or you will endure pains you can never feel but with our hands. Kill yourself or we will hound you down and rip you, all your friends, and all your family into small pieces.

We have no sympathy in killing humans who have no respect for other people's lives. Now that the slate has been cleaned and you have the world's attention, the question is what are you going to do? Are you going to admit the truth or are you going to stand resolute on your mission to eternally fuck the Weak and the Defenseless and lie about it?

Are you still going to use your power and manipulate the truth to end up with some sort of profit as you have always done?

Are you going to skip over all the crimes you've committed and act as victims to the world so you can suck in millions of donation money to turn the situation into a profit? Your two million dollar house wasn't enough? Your BMW wasn't enough? Your inheritances weren't enough?

You have to fuck and steal form the Poor and the Weak who have nothing in order to gratify your fucking pride and hedonism? What are you going to do with the blood money? Buy a new Mercedes? You want to brainwash your bratty, snobby kids that its right to steal from the poor, the Weak, and the Defenseless to always stay in power?

The fat surpluses that you roll on everyday aren't enough? Fuck you. Your answer rings loud and clear. I saw we take up the cross, Children of Ishmael, take up our guns and knives and any sharp objects, and take no prisoners and spare no lives until our last breath and last ounce of energy.

The blood of the Innocents should never be shed, but the wicked we shall spread our wings and strike. We do not want the Weak, the Defenseless, or the Innocent, but the sadistic, the corrupt, and the wicked who prey and rape from the Weak, the Defenseless, and the Innocent. We will seek and demolish them until our last breath.

You Lifetakers may have succeeded in raping our souls and shattering our dreams but mark our words the vendetta you have witnessed today will reverberate throughout every home and every soul in America and will inspire the Innocent kids that you have fucked to start a war of vendetta.

We will raise hell on earth that the world has never witnessed. Millions of deaths and millions of gallons of blood on the streets will not quench the avenging phoenix that you have caused us to unleash.

Generation after generation, we martyrs, like Eric and Dylan, will sacrifice our lives to fuck you thousand folds for what you Apostles of Sin have done to us. Pain of every atom between air and water, sky and ground, heaven and hell, life and death wouldn't begin to explain the experience that we went through under your wrath.

What did you expect me to do, you violators of human rights? As the time approached, I wished for a last minute miracle and discard this mission you've given me. Heaven knows I wouldn't hurt a single leaf of a flower. But when the time came, I did it. I had to. What other choices did you give me? All this time. You never know that a human being is capable of doing until you fuck him to the edge.

When you're raped of everything, you got nothing to lose. If you have a single milligram of conscience, a grain of integrity, a speck of heart, you will kill yourself for all the lives you have brutally extinguished.

Can you now see all that used to be, all that could have been, and all that is to come, you Sadistic Charlatans. All of you who have ever been fucked by these Descendants of Satan Disguised as Devout Christians, all of you who have went through what I went through, all of you who have felt what I have felt in my life, all of you who have suffered the wrath of these Democratic Terrorists, all of you who have been beaten, humiliated, and crucified — Children of Ishmael, Crusaders of Anti-Terrorism, my Jesus Christ Brothers and Sisters — you're in my heart.

In life and death and spirit. We'll soon be together. Let the revolution begin! Die you Descendants of Satan! Fuck you, and die now! I am Ax Ishmael. I am the Anti-Terrorist of America.

Are you happy now that you have destroyed my life? Now that you have stolen everything you could from me? Now that you have gone on a 9/11 on my life like fucking Osama. Now that you have fucked your own people like fucking Kim Jong-Il. Now that you have gone on a hummer safari on my life like fucking Bush? Are you happy now?

THE ZODIAC KILLER

Various Writings

The following pages are taken from a series of letters written by The Zodiac Killer.

During his killing spree in the 1960's and 70's these types of letters were regularly mailed to various media outlets. The poor spelling and grammar from the original Zodiac letters is included in these transcripts.

The Zodiac Murders remain unsolved to this day.

July 31st, 1969

Dear Editor

This is the murderer of the 2 teenagers last Christmass at Lake Herman + the girl on the 4th of July near the golf course in Vallejo

To prove I killed them I shall state some facts which only I + the police know.

Christmass

1 Brand name of ammo Super X

2 10 shots were fired

3 the boy was on his back with his feet to the car

4 the girl was on her right side feet to the west

4th July

1 girl was wearing paterned slacks

2 The boy was also shot in the knee.

3 Brand name of ammo was western OVER

Here is part of a cipher the other 2 parts of this cipher are being mailed to the editors of the Vallejo Times + SF Examiner.

I want you to print this cipher on the front page of your paper. In this cipher is my idenity.

If you do not print this cipher by the afternoon of Fry.1st of Aug 69, I will go on a kill ram-Page Fry. night. I will cruse around all weekend killing lone people in the night then move on to kill again, untill I end up with a dozen people over the weekend.

August 4th, 1969

Dear Editor

This is the Zodiac speaking.

In answer to your asking for more details about the good times I have had in Vallejo, I shall be very happy to supply even more material. By the way, are the police haveing a good time with the code? If not, tell them to cheer up; when they do crack it they will have me.

On the 4th of July:

I did not open the car door, The window was rolled down all ready. The boy was origionaly sitting in the front seat when I began fireing. When I fired the first shot at his head, he leaped backwards at the same time thus spoiling my aim. He ended up on the back seat then the floor in back thashing out very violently with his legs; thats how I shot him in the knee. I did not leave the cene of the killing with squealling tires + raceing engine as described in the Vallejo paper,. I drove away quite slowly so as not to draw attention to my car. The man who told the police that my car was brown was a negro about 40-45 rather shabbly dressed. I was at this phone booth haveing some fun with the Vallejo cops when he was walking by. When I hung the phone up the dam X@ thing began to ring & that drew his attention to me + my car.

Last Christmass

In that epasode the police were wondering as to how I could shoot + hit my victoms in the dark. They did not openly state this, but implied this by saying it was a well lit night + I could see the silowets on the horizon. Bullshit that area is srounded by high hills + trees. What I did was tape a small pencel flash light to the barrel of my gun.

If you notice, in the center of the beam of light if you aim it at a wall or celling you will see a black or darck spot in the center of the circle of light about 3 to 6 inches across.

When taped to a gun barrel, the bullet will strike exactly in the center of the black dot in the light. All I had to do was spray them as if it was a water hose; there was no need to use the gun sights. I was not happy to see that I did not get front page coverage.

September 27th, 1969

This is the Zodiac speaking.

I am the murderer of the taxi driver over by Washington St + Maple St last night, to prove this here is a blood stained piece of his shirt. I am the same man who did in the people in the north bay area.

The S.F. Police could have caught me last night if they had searched the park properly instead of holding road races with their motorcicles seeing who could make the most noise. The car drivers should have just parked their cars and sat there quietly waiting for me to come out of cover.

School children make nice targets, I think I shall wipe out a school bus some morning. Just shoot out the front tire + then pick off the kiddies as they come bouncing out.

November 8th, 1969

This is the Zodiac speaking

I though you would need a good laugh before you hear the bad news you won't get the news for a while yet

PS could you print this new cipher on your frunt page? I get awfully lonely when I am ignored, so lonely I could do my Thing!!!!!!

Des July Aug Sept Oct = 7

November 8th, 1969

This is the Zodiac speaking

up to the end of Oct I have killed 7 people. I have grown rather angry with the police for their telling lies about me. So I shall change the way the collecting of slaves. I shall no longer announce to anyone.

When I committ my murders, they shall look like routine robberies, killings of anger, + a few fake accidents, etc. The police shall never catch me, because I have been too clever for them.

1 I look like the description passed out only when I do my thing, the rest of the time I look entirle different. I shall not tell you what my descise consists of when I kill

2 As of yet I have left no fingerprints behind me contrary to what the police say in my killings I wear transparent fingertip guards. All it is is 2 coats of airplane cement coated on my fingertips -- quite unnoticible + very efective

3 my killing tools have been boughten through the mail order outfits before the ban went into efect. Except one & it was bought out of the state. So as you can see the police don't have much to work on.

If you wonder why I was wipeing the cab down I was leaving fake clews for the police to run all over town with, as one might say, I gave the cops som bussy work to do to keep them happy. I enjoy needling the blue pigs. Hey blue pig I was in the park -- you were useing fire trucks to mask the sound of your cruzeing prowl cars. The dogs never came with in 2 blocks of me + they were to the west + there was only 2 groups of parking about 10 min apart then the motor cicles went by about 150 ft away going from south to north west

p.s. 2 cops pulled a goof abot 3 min after I left the cab. I was walking down the hill to the park when this cop car pulled up + one of them called me over + asked if I saw anyone acting suspicious or strange in the last 5 to 10 min + I said yes there was this man who was runnig by waveing a gun & the cops peeled rubber + went around the corner as I directed them + I disappeared into the park a block + a half away never to be seen again. "must print in paper."

Hey pig doesnt it rile you up to have your noze rubed in your booboos? If you cops think I'm going to take on a bus the way I stated I was, you deserve to have holes in your heads. Take one bag of ammonium nitrate fertilizer + 1 gal of stove oil & dump a few bags of gravel on top + then set the shit off + will positivily ventalate any thing that should be in the way of the blast.

The death machine is all ready made. I would have sent you pictures but you would be nasty enough to trace them back to developer + then to me, so I shall describe my masterpiece to you.

The nice part of it is all the parts can be bought on the open market with no questions asked.

1 bat. Pow clock -- will run for aprox 1 year
1 photoelectric switch
2 copper leaf springs
2 6V car bat
1 flash light bulb + reflector
1 mirror
2 18" cardboard tubes black with shoe polish inside + oute
Mirror
bus
Bombs (1 bag each)
6V Bat
6V Bat
bus goes bang car
pass es by ok.

The system checks out from one end to the other in my tests.

What you do not know is whether the death machine is at the sight or whether it is being stored in my basement for future use. I think you do not have the manpower to stop this one by continually searching the road sides looking for this thing. + it wont do to re roat + re schedule the busses because the bomb can be adapted to new conditions.

Have fun!! By the way it could be rather messy if you try to bluff me.

PS. Be shure to print the part I marked out on page 3 or I shall do my thing.

To prove that I am the Zodiac, Ask the Vallejo cop about my electric gun sight which I used to start my collecting of slaves.

CHRISTOPHER DORNER

Manifesto Excerpt

On Feburary 3rd, 2013, former police officer Christopher Dorner began a killing spree to protest what he described as inherent racism and unchecked police brutality within the Los Angeles Police Department. Four were murdered and three injured by Dorner.

During the manhunt, the LAPD and Torrence P.D. injured three innocent people in shooting incidents after mistakenly identifying citizens as Dorner.

The following is a segment of the manifesto Dorner published online in an attempt to explain his actions. The names of the accused have been redacted.

From: Christopher Jordan Dorner /7648
To: America
Subj: Last resort
Regarding CF# 07-004281

I know most of you who personally know me are in disbelief to hear from media reports that I am suspected of committing such horrendous murders and have taken drastic and shocking actions in the last couple of days. You are saying to yourself that this is completely out of character of the man you knew who always wore a smile wherever he was seen.

I know I will be vilified by the LAPD and the media. Unfortunately, this is a necessary evil that I do not enjoy but must partake and complete for substantial change to occur within the LAPD and reclaim my name. The department has not changed since the Rampart and Rodney King days. It has gotten worse. The consent decree should never have been lifted. The only thing that has evolved from the consent decree is those officers involved in the Rampart scandal and Rodney King incidents have since promoted to supervisor, commanders, and command staff, and executive positions.

The question is, what would you do to clear your name?

Name;
A word or set of words by which a person, animal, place, or thing is known, addressed, or referred to.

Name
Synonyms;
reputation, title, appellation, denomination, repute.

A name is more than just a noun, verb, or adjective. It's your life, your legacy, your journey, sacrifices, and everything you've worked hard for every day of your life as and adolescent, young adult and adult. Don't let anybody tarnish it when you know you've live up to your own set of ethics and personal ethos.

In 8/07 I reported an officer (Ofcr. ——-/now a Sergeant), for kicking a suspect (excessive force) during a Use of Force while I was assigned as a patrol officer at LAPD's Harbor Division. While cuffing the suspect, (——-), ——- kicked the suspect twice in the chest and once in the face.

The kick to the face left a visible injury on the left cheek below the eye. Unfortunately after reporting it to supervisors and investigated by PSB (internal affairs investigator Det. ——-), nothing was done. I had broken their supposed "Blue Line". Unfortunately, It's not JUST US, it's JUSTICE!!!

In fact, 10 months later on 6/25/08, after already successfully completing probation, acquiring a basic Post Certificate, and Intermediate Post Certificate, I was relieved of duty by the LAPD while assigned to patrol at Southwest division. It is clear as day that the department retaliated toward me for reporting ——- for kicking Mr. ——-.

The department stated that I had lied and made up the report that ——- had kicked the suspect. I later went to a Board of Rights (department hearing for decision of continued employment) from 10/08 to 1/09. During this BOR hearing a video was played for the BOR panel where ——- stated that he was indeed kicked by Officer ——- (video sent to multiple news agencies). In addition to ——- stating he was kicked, his father ——-, also stated that his son had stated he was kicked by an officer when he was arrested after being released from custody.

This was all presented for the department at the BOR hearing. They still found me guilty and terminated me. What they didn't mention was that the BOR panel made up of Capt. ——-, Capt. ——-, and City Attorney ——- had a significant problem from the time the board was assembled. Capt. ——- was a personal friend of ——- from when he was her supervisor at Harbor station.

That is a clear conflict of interest and I made my argument for his removal early and was denied. The advocate for the LAPD BOR was Sgt. ——-. ——- also had a conflict of interest as she was ——- friend and former partner from Harbor division where they both worked patrol together.

I made my argument for her removal when I discovered her relation to ——- and it was denied.

During the BOR, the department attempted to label me unsuccessfully as a bully.

They stated that I had bullied a recruit, ——-, in the academy when in reality and unfounded disposition from the official 1.28 formal complaint investigation found that I was the one who stood up for ——- when other recruits sang nazi hitler youth songs about burning Jewish ghettos in WWII Germany where his father was a survivor of a concentration camp.

How fucking dare you attempt to label me with such a nasty vile word. I ask that all earnest journalist investigating this story ask Ofcr. ——- about the incident when Ofcr. ——- began singing a nazi youth song about burning jewish ghettos.

The internal affairs investigation in the academy involving ——- was spurned by a complaint that I had initiated toward two fellow recruit/offifcers. While assigned patrol footbeat in Hollywood Division, Officers ——- and ——- (both current LAPD officers) decided that they would voice their personal feelings about the black community.

While traveling back to the station in a 12 passenger van I heard ——- refer to another individual as a nigger. I wasn't sure if I heard correctly as there were many conversations in the van that was compiled of at least 8 officers and he was sitting in the very rear and me in the very front.

Even with the multiple conversations and ambient noise I heard Officer ——- call an indivdual a nigger again. Now that I had confirmed it, I told ——- not to use that word again.

I explained that it was a well-known offensive word that should not be used by anyone. He replied, “I’ll say it when I want”. Officer ——-, a friend of his, also stated that he would say nigger when he wanted. At that point I jumped over my front passenger seat and two other officers where I placed my hands around ——-’ neck and squeezed.

I stated to ——-, “Don’t fucking say that”. At that point there was pushing and shoving and we were separated by several other officers. What I should have done, was put a Winchester Ranger SXT 9mm 147 grain bullet in his skull and Officer ——-’s skull. The Situation would have been resolved effective, immediately.

The sad thing about this incident was that when Detective ——- from internal affairs investigated this incident only (1) officer (unknown) in the van other than myself had statements constistent with what actually happened.

The other six officers all stated they heard nothing and saw nothing. Shame on every one of you. Shame on Detective ——- (same ethnicity as ——-) for creating a separate 1.28 formal complaint against me (——-complaint) in retaliation for initiating the complaint against ——- and ——-.

Don’t retaliate against honest officers for breaking your so-called blue line. I hope your son ——-, who I knew, is a better officer than you, Detective ——-. The saddest part of this ordeal was that Officer ——- and

——- were only given 22 day suspensions and are still LAPD officers to this day. That day, the LAPD stated that it is acceptable for fellow officers to call black officers niggers to their face and you will receive a slap on the wrist.

Even sadder is that during that 22 day suspension ——- and ——- received is that the LAPPL (Los Angeles Police Protective League) paid the officers their salaries while they were suspended. When I took a two-day suspension for an accidental discharge, I took my suspension and never applied for a league salary. Its called integrity.

Journalist, I want you to investigate every location I resided in growing up. Find any incidents where I was ever accused of being a bully. You won't, because it doesn't exist. It's not in my DNA. Never was. I was the only black kid in each of my elementary school classes from first grade to seventh grade in junior high and any instances where I was disciplined for fighting was in response to fellow students provoking common childhood schoolyard fights, or calling me a nigger or other derogatory racial names.

I grew up in neighborhoods where blacks make up less than 1%. My first recollection of racism was in the first grade at Norwalk Christian elementary school in Norwalk, CA. A fellow student, ——- if I can recall, called me a nigger on the playground. My response was swift and non-lethal.

I struck him fast and hard with a punch an kick. He cried and reported it to a teacher. The teacher reported it to the principal. The principal swatted ——- for using a derogatory word toward me. He then for some unknown reason swatted me for striking ——- in response to him calling me a nigger.

He stated as good Christians we are to turn the other cheek as Jesus did. Problem is, I'm not a fucking Christian and that old book, made of fiction and limited non-fiction, called the bible, never once stated Jesus was called a nigger. How dare you swat me for standing up for my rights for demanding that I be treated as an equal human being.

That day I made a life decision that i will not tolerate racial derogatory terms spoken to me. Unfortunately I was swatted multiple times for the same exact reason up until junior high. Terminating me for telling the truth of a Caucasian officer kicking a mentally ill man is disgusting.

Don't ever call me a fucking bully. I want all journalist to utilize every source you have that specializes in collections for your reports. With the discovery and evidence available you will see the truth. Unfortunately, I will not be alive to see my name cleared. That's what this is about, my name.

A man is nothing without his name.

10468597R00149

Printed in Great Britain
by Amazon